TRANSITION WORDS
with Your Team

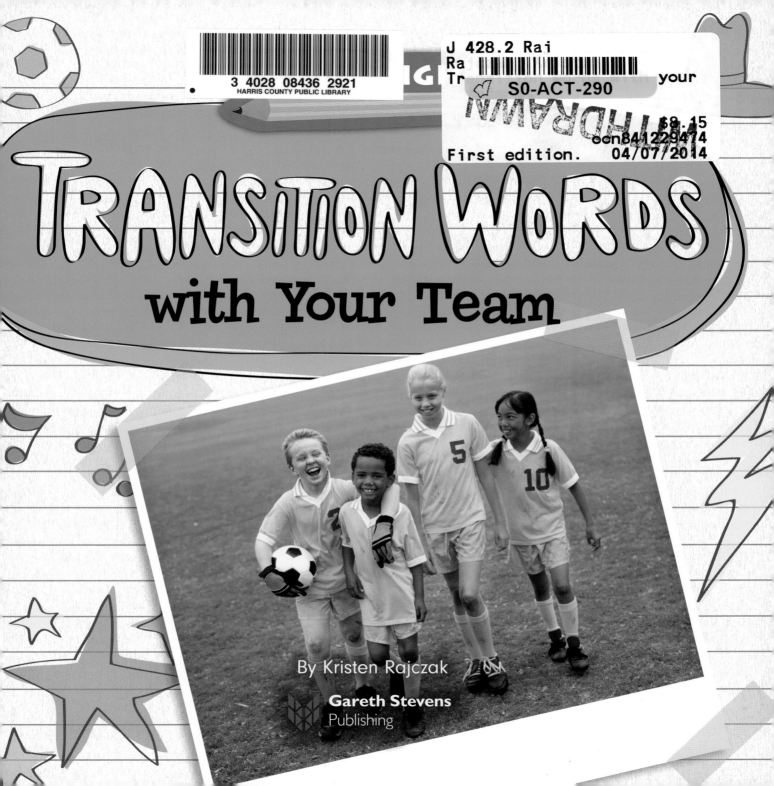

By Kristen Rajczak

Gareth Stevens
Publishing

Please visit our website, www.garethstevens.com. For a free color catalog of all our high-quality books, call toll free 1-800-542-2595 or fax 1-877-542-2596.

Library of Congress Cataloging-in-Publication Data

Rajczak, Kristen.
Transition words with your team / by Kristen Rajczak.
    p. cm. — (Write right!)
Includes index.
ISBN 978-1-4339-9086-1 (pbk.)
ISBN 978-1-4339-9087-8 (6-pack)
ISBN 978-1-4339-9085-4 (library binding)
1. English language — Sentences — Juvenile literature. 2. English language — Terms and phrases — Juvenile literature. 3. English language — Grammar — Juvenile literature. I. Rajczak, Kristen. II. Title.
PE1441.R35 2014
428.2—d23

First Edition

Published in 2014 by
Gareth Stevens Publishing
111 East 14th Street, Suite 349
New York, NY 10003

Designer: Sarah Liddell
Editor: Kristen Rajczak

Photo credits: Cover, p. 1 Stockbyte/Thinkstock.com; p. 5 Monkey Business Images/Shutterstock.com; p. 7 Ty Allison/Photographer's Choice/Getty Images; p. 9 © iStockphoto.com/asiseeit; p. 11 nicole waring/Vetta/Getty Images; p. 13 © iStockphoto.com/kali9; p. 15 Fuse/Getty Images; p. 17 Big Cheese Photo/Thinkstock.com; p. 19 Enrico Calderoni/Getty Images.

Printed in the United States of America

CPSIA compliance information: Batch #CS13GS: For further information contact Gareth Stevens, New York, New York at 1-800-542-2595.

CONTENTS

Words in the glossary appear in **bold** type the first time they are used in the text.

WHAT'S A TRANSITION?

After a big game, you'll want to tell your family and friends how your team won! In order to do so, you'll need to use transition words.

Transition words help a piece of writing flow more smoothly. They provide **organization** and show change. Transition words act as **signals** to the reader about the connection between sentences or ideas.

There are many kinds of transition words. Some you might be familiar with include however, moreover, before, and for example.

ON THE WRITE TRACK

Trans- in the word "transition" means "change."

Writers use transition words to make their writing more interesting and orderly.

5

TELL ME MORE

One important reason writers use transition words is to signal continuation or the addition of more information. Transition words of addition include **additionally**, **also**, and **as well as**.

Von has been a **sprinter** on the outdoor track team for 2 years. **Additionally**, he's the team's best long jumper.

Christina joined the track team because she likes to run. **Also**, she's fast!

Jossie runs long-distance events on the cross-country team **as well as** shorter races for the track-and-field team.

ON THE WRITE TRACK

Transition words are used both between sentences and within a sentence to show the connection between ideas.

Other transition words that show information will be added are **besides**, **furthermore**, and **moreover**.

WHEN WAS THAT?

Sequential words are transitions that tell when something happened. They show in what order events occurred, too. This is especially important when talking about sports!

Yesterday, Pierre and Lucy played in a soccer game. **At the beginning**, Pierre passed the ball to Lucy. **Then**, she ran down the field. **Suddenly**, a player from the other team tried to steal the ball. **At the same time**, Pierre ran up behind Lucy. She passed him the ball—and he scored a goal!

ON THE WRITE TRACK

Sequential words include numerical, or number, words. First, second, and third are all numerical sequential words.

Sequential words are often considered transition words that signal the addition of information.

MORE OF THE SAME

Another group of transition words is used when comparing two sentences or ideas. Words such as **likewise**, **too**, and **in comparison** signal to the reader that the two sentences or ideas are similar.

Bernard had his skates sharpened for the start of hockey season. **Likewise**, Gene bought a new helmet.

Many players from last season wanted to play hockey again this year. Harlan, **too**, wanted to join.

In comparison to last year, Sam shoots the puck better now.

ON THE WRITE TRACK

Other transition words showing similarity are easy to remember. They include similarly and the same as.

YOU'RE OUT!

Writers may signal differences between sentences or ideas using transition words, too. Transition words of **contrast** show the sides of an argument or explain why an idea is untrue or incorrect.

Marta thought her final out in the softball game was the reason her team lost. **On the other hand**, other girls had struck out during the game, too.

Though Kurt wanted to pitch for the baseball team, he knew his broken finger wouldn't heal in time.

ON THE WRITE TRACK

In an argument, transition words such as *naturally*, *granted*, and *of course* show **concession**. That means they signal when the writer admits that a point made in the argument is true, even if it's a point made by the other side.

Many other words signal contrast. **However**, **but at the same time**, and **despite** are just a few more.

GIVE A REASON

Do you want to explain why you missed a jump shot? Transition words that show cause and effect can help! The most common transition word showing cause is **because**.

Because it was raining, the basketball team practiced in the gym instead of on the outdoor court.

Transition words signaling effect, or consequence, include **as a result**, **for this reason**, and **therefore**.

As Jackson neared the basket, a player on the other team got in his way. **For this reason**, Jackson passed the ball instead of shooting.

ON THE WRITE TRACK

Cause-and-effect words let the reader know a change will happen.

Actions and reactions are an important part of sports, so words that show cause and effect are important for writing about playing with your team.

15

ONE MORE TRICK

Giving an example further explains something you've written. There are many transition words that signal an example will follow. **For instance, for example**, and **such as** are some of the most common.

The cheerleading squad, or team, has many talented members. **For example**, both Alissa and Chelsey can do front flips and backflips. The squad knows other gymnastics moves **such as** splits, cartwheels, and jumps. They perform often. **For instance**, they cheer for the football team every week in the fall.

ON THE WRITE TRACK

When repeating information or giving a sentence or idea **emphasis**, writers can use transition words like most of all, in fact, to repeat, or in other words.

Examples add detail to a piece of writing, which makes it more interesting!

IN CONCLUSION

Often, the most exciting part of a sports matchup is the end. Certain transition words can signal to the reader that the end is coming.

Darryl's golf team was losing, but not by much. **Finally**, he was up—and hit a hole in one to win!

The tennis match went on for more than an hour! **In the end**, Jessica scored the winning point.

Transition words signal summary, too. Use **to sum up**, **in short**, and **altogether** for this.

ON THE WRITE TRACK

In general, usually, and on the whole are examples of transitions that signal to the reader that a **generalization** will follow. These are similar to words of summary.

Transition words can be used to signal the end of a story, but they also can signal the end of an argument or idea.

19

GAME RECAP

Transition words are useful when writing about sports! The transitions in the paragraph below are highlighted.

Last week, Alec's soccer team had a big game. The team planned to pass the ball a lot **because** they wanted to tire out the other team with tons of running. **Though** Alec was the fastest player, he was guarding the goal. So, Jake was in Alec's usual position. **While** some players were worried Jake wouldn't play well, **in the end** they were happy. Jake scored two goals!

ON THE WRITE TRACK

A paragraph is a collection of sentences all dealing with one idea. Writers often use transition words between paragraphs to move smoothly between two ideas.

WHEN TO USE TRANSITION WORDS

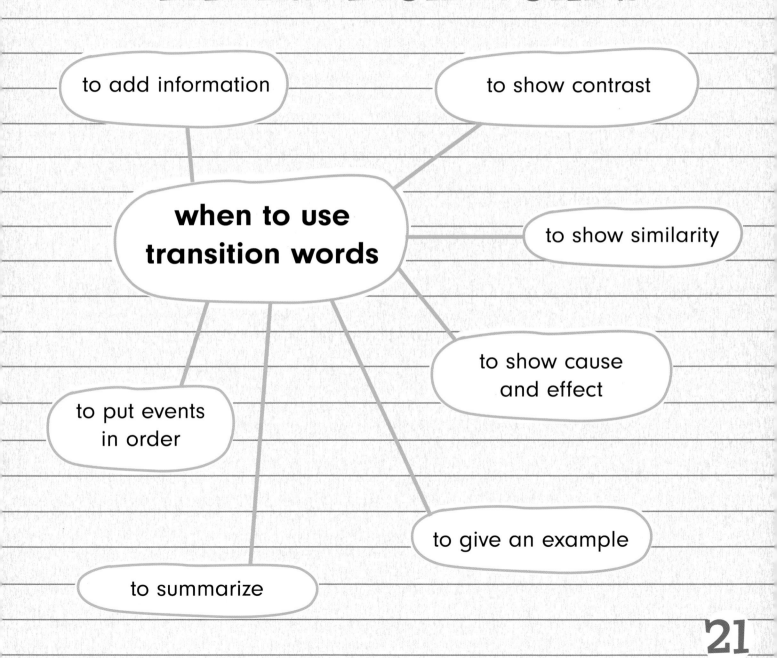

to add information

to show contrast

when to use transition words

to show similarity

to put events in order

to show cause and effect

to summarize

to give an example

GLOSSARY

concession: agreeing with a point claimed in an argument

contrast: difference

emphasis: special importance given to something

generalization: the act of stating a general conclusion

organization: the order of something

reaction: response

signal: a sign or action that lets someone know something. Also, the use of the sign or action.

sprinter: someone who runs very fast for a short period of time

FOR MORE INFORMATION

BOOKS

Riggs, Ann. *Sentence Types and Punctuation*. Mankato, MN: Creative Education, 2012.

Terban, Marvin. *Scholastic Guide to Grammar*. New York, NY: Scholastic, 2010.

WEBSITES

How to Use Transition Words and Phrases in an Essay
www.bookrags.com/articles/11.html
Read tips for using transitions in a longer piece of writing.

Transitional Words and Phrases
www.mun.ca/writingcentre/docs/OnLineTransitionalWords.pdf
Review your knowledge of transitions using this helpful document.

INDEX